JIM-JAM PYJAMAS

JIM-JAM PYJAMAS

Gina Wilson

*Illustrated by
Sally Anne Lambert*

JONATHAN CAPE
LONDON

First published 1990
This collection text © Gina Wilson 1990
Illustrations © Sally Anne Lambert 1990
Jonathan Cape Ltd, 20 Vauxhall Bridge Road, London SW1V 2SA

A CIP catalogue record for this book
is available from the British Library

"Jim-Jam Pyjamas" was first published in
Ducks and Dragons, Faber 1980, and "Proud
Peacock" in *The Times Literary Supplement*,
October 1981

ISBN 0 224 02676 3

Typeset at The Spartan Press Ltd
Lymington, Hants
Printed in Great Britain by
Butler & Tanner Ltd
Frome and London

For Edward

Contents

Jim-Jam Pyjamas	9
Cross Canary	10
Ice Pact	11
Hippy Hippo	12
Please!	14
Midnight Steed	16
Skiver!	18
Madame Giraffe	19
Old Pal	20
Water Sport	21
First Breath of Winter	22
Name Game	23
Superswan	24
Don't Blame the Bird!	25
Monkey Business	26
A Song for Winter	28
Walking Pyramid – or Dromedary	29
The Weeper	30
Don't . . .	31
Hagwitch	32
King Fish	33
Special Bear	34
Red Alert	35
Mad Kangaroo	36
Proud Peacock	39
Cat	40
Cool Camel	42
Index of First Lines	45

Jim-Jam Pyjamas

He wears striped jim-jam pyjamas,
You never saw jim-jams like those –
A fine-fitting, stretchy, fur cat-suit,
Skin-tight from his head to his toes.

He wears striped jim-jam pyjamas,
Black and yellow and dashingly gay;
He makes certain that everyone sees them
By keeping them on all the day.

He wears striped jim-jam pyjamas,
He walks with a smug-pussy stride;
There's no hiding his pride in his jim-jams
With their zig-zaggy lines down each side.

He wears striped jim-jam pyjamas
And pauses at times to display
The effect as he flexes his torso –
Then he fancies he hears people say:

"I wish I had jim-jam pyjamas!
I wish I were feline and slim!
Oh, look at that brave Bengal tiger!
Oh, how I should love to be him!"

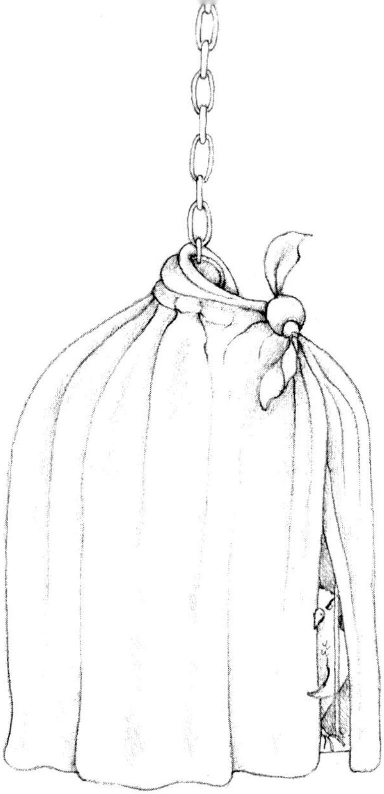

Cross Canary

He sings when he's happy,
He sings when he's sad,
He sings when he's middling,
But not when he's mad.

He's not singing now
'Cause Mum's covered his cage
With a blanket for bedtime
And he's in a rage.

Ice Pact

Oh-so-sober Polar Bear,
Snowy face, snowy hair,
Is it because our sun's too hot
You growl a lot?

Oh-so-sober Polar Bear,
Plodding here, plodding there,
Is it because you think you'll melt
In that pelt?

Oh-so-sober Polar Bear,
Winter's near, don't despair –
There'll be snow, there'll be ice,
In a trice.

Then I'll come, Polar Bear,
And when I stand, when I stare,
You will know I'm just like you –
Frozen through!

Hippy Hippo

I lost my heart to a hippo
In an animal park in Tyrone;
He was basking in steamy, green waters,
I was wandering there alone.

His scrubbing-brush lips fell a-sighing,
He tipped me a watery wink –
Like the rainbow burst of a bubble
Of soap in a kitchen sink.

His rubber-bung ears started hopping
Like frogs on a wet afternoon,
And he crooned me a 'potamus love-lilt
In a voice like a bass bassoon:

"Come, jump in my whirlpool beside me!
Come, join me in life's giddy swim!"
Then he plunged beneath the foul wavelets,
And my heart plunged after him.

Still echoed his voice from the mud-bed
Like the boom of a foghorn at sea:
"Come, paddle-dy-wallow, my Pretty!
Come, paddle-dy-wallow with me!"

My heart ached beside the green waters;
"If I were a hippo," I cried,
"I'd paddle-dy-wallow, my Handsome,
For ever, with you at my side!"

Please!

Elegant lady house mouse
With ears of delicate rose,
Tripping your way from room to room
On dainty pointed toes,

Nobody seems to like you –
You're a most unwelcome guest;
Mother's in tears you've stayed so long
And Father calls you a pest.

Oh, please, won't you move into my room
And sleep on the spare divan?
I'll bring you nuts in a silver dish
And slices of marzipan,

And pieces of cheese in fancy shapes
And cups of China tea.
I know you like to be secret –
Come and be secret with me.

Midnight Steed

He trembles there among the trees,
Waiting – half in, half out, of sight –
Among the dancing, prancing leaves,
My midnight steed of black and white.

Dusk falls and, in that fleeting space
'Twixt day and night, I see him plain –
His satin stripes of dark and light,
His whispering hooves, his bounding mane.

Deep in the night, beneath the moon,
He canters clear and lifts his face;
Through tangled skeins of dreams I speed
To join him in the Midnight Place.

Together, over velvet plains
Of summer skies, we gallop free –
Where midnight steeds alone can go,
And only midnight riders see . . .

I never know what brings us back,
Or why he vanishes with dawn;
Each morn I wake alone and find,
Unchanged, outside, our empty lawn . . .

But, all day long, I know he's there,
My midnight steed of black and white,
Among those dancing, prancing leaves,
Waiting – half in, half out, of sight.

Skiver!

Crafty cuckoo lays her egg
In someone else's nest,
Then frolics off to freedom
While they do all the rest!

Madame Giraffe

I've seen the tallest lady –
She's like a walking crane!
Her neck is like a steeple
And her head's the weather-vane!

Or else it's like a ladder
Propped up against a wall,
And from the top she peers down
And we look very small!

Some people think she's snooty
With her nose stuck in the sky;
But I expect she's lonely
Up aloft, and shy.

The sparrows say she's beautiful –
Only the sparrows know!
What a waste of beauty
Not to let it show!

I'm going to coax her gently
– She knows I understand –
One day, she'll bend her head right down
And eat out of my hand.

Old Pal

My labrador grew blind and grey;
He lay beneath the tree all day
Where once we used to play.

At dusk I sat out there as well;
I stroked him while the shadows fell;
He knew me by my smell.

I buried him beneath the tree;
Each day I go there after tea;
I know he knows it's me.

Water Sport

Super smooth and super cool!
Hero of the swimming-pool!

>Ace-cavorter!
>Water-snorter!

>Skiver! Jiver!
>Sky-high-diver!

Whiskery, friskery,
Taking a riskery!

>Blubbery, scrubbery,
>Rub-a-dub-dubbery!

Flippery, flappery,
Clappy slap-happery!

>Splishery, sploshery,
>Black macintoshery. . . !

I wish I had a wet-suit too
So I could water-sport with you!

But don't you sometimes want to be
Snug . . . and warm . . . and *dry* – like ME?

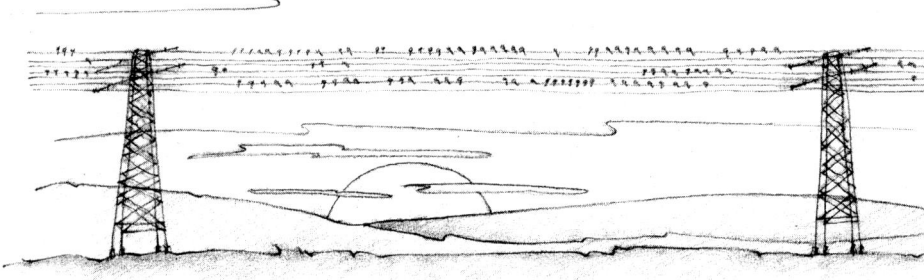

First Breath of Winter

Like autumn leaves, tossed high
In a fickle sky,
You fly, Swallows.

Reckless, you dart,
Urged to depart
By that bluff puff –
You pierce my heart.

I loved you when you came, glad-swooping
Out of Heaven, looping
Long-tailed streamers;
I love you yet . . .

But soon, at sunset,
All along the miles of wire and fence,
You'll sit in whispering rows,
Till the next puff blows
You hence.

Name Game

The ugliest animal on earth
Endures a double woe:
Not only is he ugly,
But his name reminds us so!

If we had called the WARTHOG
By a more appealing name,
He might have seemed appealing,
Though his looks remained the same.

Superswan

I do not like the way you walk;
Walking is not for you!
You're for the unmapped wastes of sky,
The unswum deeps of blue.

Not for you the common clay
That clogs our common feet;
You're for that otherworldly space
Where air and waters meet.

Don't stagger on your stubby pins,
Don't roll like a drunken tar!
Soar, with a surge of snowy pens,
Up where the planets are!

And when, over all, your last lone call
Trembles, and day is done,
Glide, like a full-rigged galleon,
Into the dying sun.

Don't Blame the Bird!

My Aunt Ethelberta's parrot
Is a genius of a bird:
It comes out with strings of language
She insists it's never heard –
Drunkards' oaths, and sailors' curses,
Swearwords that a harassed nurse is
Bound to utter if she drops
A bedpan or a pail of slops . . .
Mum makes me block my ears up fast
When Polly starts to "damn" and "blast".
She begs me never once to speak
The words that issue from that beak.
Aunt Ethelberta looks demure –
"He's not learnt that from me, I'm sure.
However blue may be my mood,
I never let my talk get crude."
Then Father turns to wink an eye,
Breathing, "In that case, tell me why
Polly always makes the choice
To swear in Ethelberta's voice!"

Monkey Business

I had a chimpanzee once –
He played the violin.
I put him on the London stage,
And watched the crowds roll in.

They flocked to see his monkey-tricks
With Brahms and Berlioz;
Sometimes he balanced on his hands
And fiddled with his toes.

He wore a suit from Savile Row
Over his monkey skin,
With tails to cover up his tail
And bows beneath his chin.

I gave him yams and coconuts
And fruit of the baobab tree;
He didn't like the taste of cash
So he gave that to me!

I lived like a queen with a limousine,
I flew by private jet –
Till he lost his head, and up and wed
A tinker's marmoset!

He packed his fiddle, and left in the middle
Of a coal-black, starless night,
And now I'm poor as I was before;
I suppose that serves me right . . .

I loved my chimpanzee, you see –
Why did I think it funny
To put him on the London stage
And collar all his money?

A Song for Winter

Banana-bill, Banana-bill,
What's that melody you trill?

Freckle-flute, again . . . again . . .
A masterpiece to woo your hen . . .

Lark, your descant dances high
Above green fields in still July;

And in the dead of night you sing,
Nightingale, with moonlit wing.

Songbirds, let me sing like you –
In tones like yours, tunes just as true.

Oh, teach me all the Summer long;
In Winter, I will sing my song.

Walking Pyramid – or Dromedary

He views us with disdainful eyes
Beneath half-shuttered lids;
We viewed him for a million years,
Then built the pyramids!

He thinks we must be somewhat dim
To take so long to copy him!

The Weeper

All alone, alone I dwell,
Captive within my bony shell,
A hermit in a hermit's cell.

I have no feet, I cannot walk;
I have no tongue, I cannot talk;
But eyes I have, each on a stalk –

Their dazzling drops of sorrow fall
In glints of silver over all,
As, silken, beneath the moon, I crawl.

Across the grass at dawn you see,
Shimmering, my tearful tracery;
No other creature weeps like me!

Don't . . .

Don't alarm a llama –
That's really most unkind;
And if you harm a llama
Its mother's bound to mind.

But if you calm a llama
That's been bullied or annoyed
You'll find that calmer llama's
Mum is overjoyed.

Hagwitch

      A coal-black crow
      With a coal-black eye,
      And a coal-black beak
      To poke and pry,
Jigged round a sheep-skull, caw-, caw-, calling,
High on a crag when night was falling.

      A coal-black crone
      With a coal-black cloak
      And a coal-black broomstick,
      Up she spoke:
"Owl's tongue, eel's eye, slime from a pigsty,
Bat's shriek, blow fly, craw of a magpie!"

      A coal-black spell
      Of cold, black death –
      To curdle blood
      And stifle breath –
Down from the crag came creep-, creep-, creeping . . .
Hark . . . in the valley, now . . . someone's weeping!

King Fish

Suspended in his liquid orb,
He flaunts his regal mail,
And stares with flat, unblinking eye,
Tossing a silken tail.

Around his round, round world he swims,
Every inch a king!
While round and round I swim in mine
And don't rule anything.

Special Bear

Who gave the panda two black eyes,
And punched him on the nose,
And boxed his ears black and blue,
And stamped upon his toes?
It's made him look a sorry sight,
Huddling in his lair,
Partly black and partly white.
"Oh, Special Chinese Bear,
I'm going to bring you bamboo shoots
And watch you crunch them to the roots:
It'll give you back a bit of pride
To know that I am on your side!"

Red Alert

Flame-tail!
Crackerjack!
Racing to the top and back!
Slim, trim,
Full of vim,
Chasing out along a limb!
Dash, dart,
Stop and start;
Dark spark
Against the bark;
Lick of red
Overhead;
Live wire
Leaping higher;
FOREST FIRE!

Mad Kangaroo

The kangaroo went on a crazy rampage –
With a hop, step and jump she leapt clear of her cage
And bounced into town in a whirlwind of haste
With her baby tucked into a pouch at her waist.

She made for the parkland and bounced on the green –
Like a grassy municipal trampoline –
And her brave little baby stuck out his bare head:
"She's a marvellous marsupial mother!" he said.

She climbed up the steeple and bounced on the top
Till the priest lost his temper and begged her to stop,
And her soft fluffy baby remarked with a sigh,
"How lucky I am that my mother can fly!"

She made for the railway and bounced down the lines
While the train drivers bellowed and made angry signs;
But her pouch with its baby was starting to sag
Like an old overloaded brown carrier-bag,

So she called it a day and bounced back to the zoo,
Ignoring the fuss and the hullaballoo,
And she said to her keeper, "I like what I do!
I'm a thumping-mad, jumping-mad, mad kangaroo!"

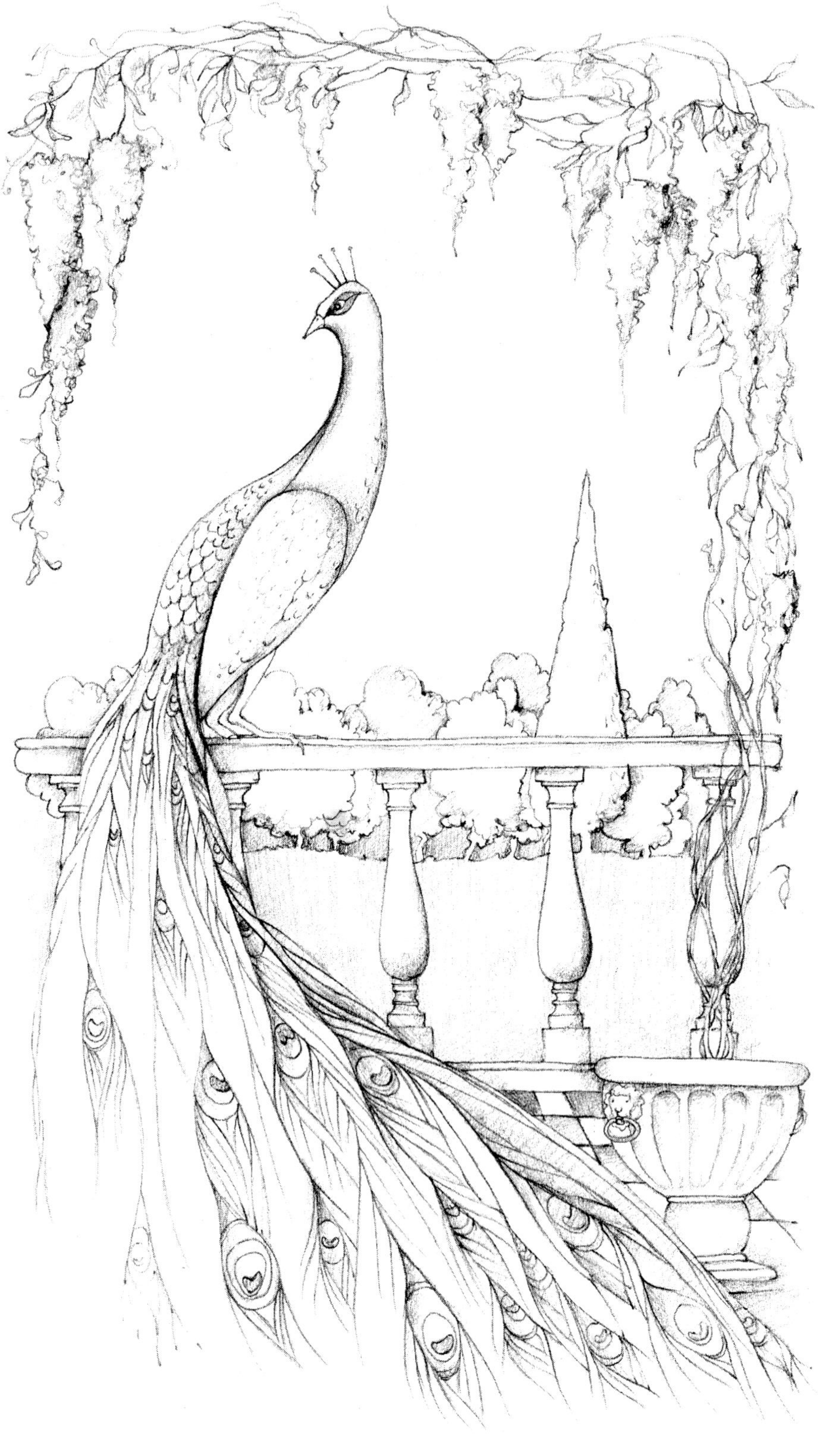

Proud Peacock

Peacock in the castle grounds,
You polished, poised and princely male,
Attended by a thousand eyes
Caught in the spreading of your tail,

Make me a member of your court,
To spice the air with odours sweet,
To fill the silver water founts
And scatter seed pearls at your feet.

Make me a member of your train,
To set agleam your plumage blue,
To tend the splendour of your fan
When you parade in public view.

And let me follow in your wake,
A dusky peahen, meek and small,
Saving the pearls you leave behind
And gathering up the plumes that fall.

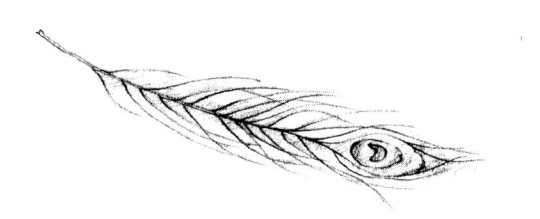

Cat

Mum couldn't stand the cat next door –
It dumped chewed corpses on *our* floor:
Mice and lice and moles and voles,
And other things that live in holes,
And birds and bats and dragon-flies,
And squashy things that have no eyes,
Like worms and slugs and snails – which all
Drove Mum, stark-staring, up the wall.

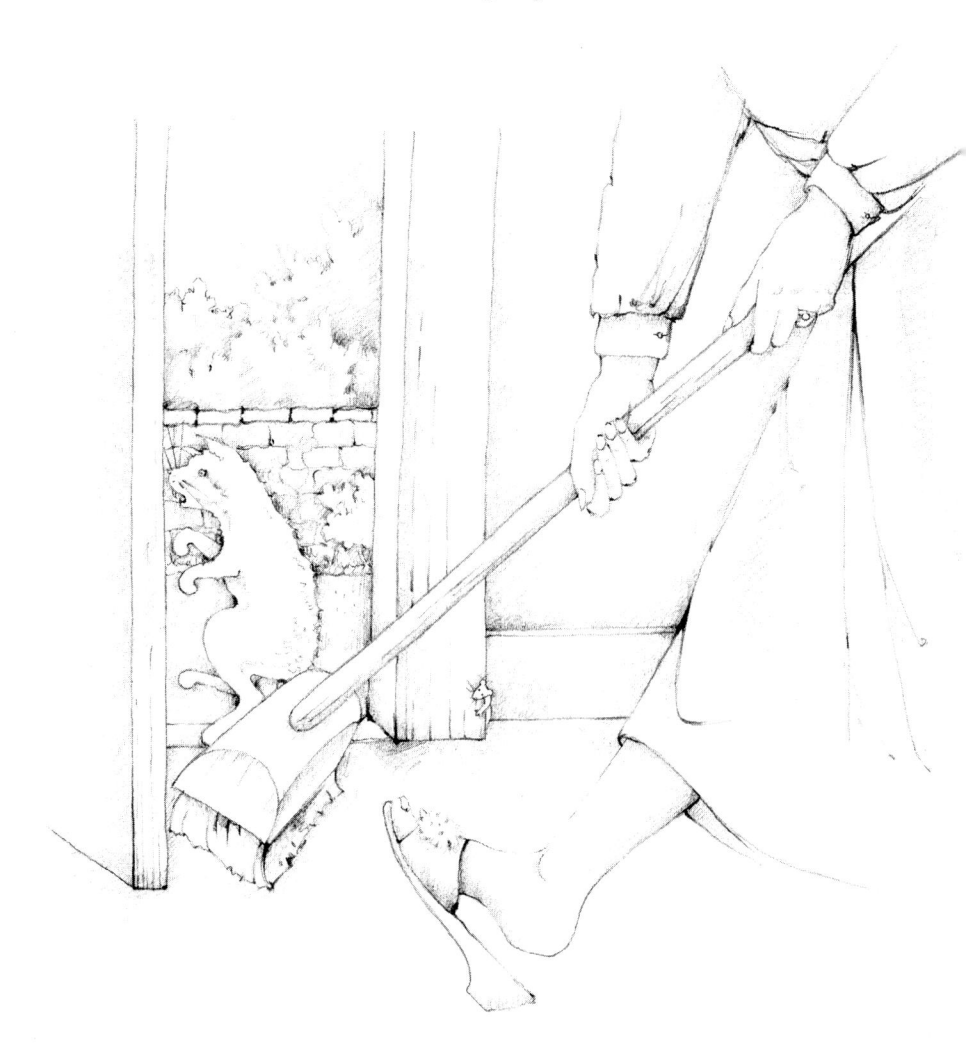

Now Dad's enticed that cat to stay
With us! He gives it cream each day,
And dace and plaice and hake and steak,
Chicken, minced, and chocolate cake;
And now the cat, all cute and twee,
Sits purring on my mother's knee!
  – It takes that other stuff next door
   And dumps it on *their* kitchen floor!

Cool Camel

Nomad Camel, with his pack
Strapped in two humps on his back,
Is off to roam the desert dry
With his outstanding food supply.

The front hump's stuffed with cake and jam,
Slices of turkey, beef and ham;
The back one's full of ale and stout
And orange-juice, against the drought.

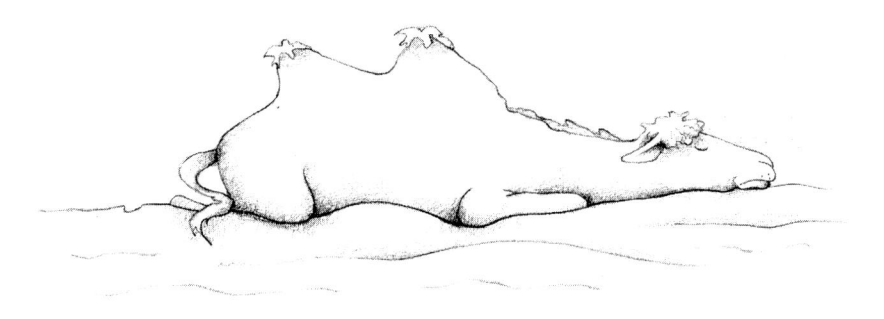

Spiked cacti lurk along his way,
Mirages lure him miles astray,
The noon sun hammers on his head,
And whirlwind sands leave him for dead.

Still, Nomad tramps his ancient track,
Dauntless, with his survival pack . . .
To where the last oasis flies
Bright flags of green against the skies!

Index of First Lines

A coal-black crow	32
All alone, alone I dwell	30
Banana-bill, Banana-bill	28
Crafty cuckoo lays her egg	18
Don't alarm a llama	31
Elegant lady house mouse	14
Flame-tail!	35
He sings when he's happy	10
He trembles there among the trees	16
He views us with disdainful eyes	29
He wears striped jim-jam pyjamas	9

I do not like the way you walk	24
I had a chimpanzee once	26
I lost my heart to a hippo	12
I've seen the tallest lady	19
Like autumn leaves, tossed high	22
Mum couldn't stand the cat next door	40
My Aunt Ethelberta's parrot	25
My labrador grew blind and grey	20
Nomad Camel, with his pack	42
Oh-so-sober Polar Bear	11
Peacock in the castle grounds	39
Super smooth and super cool!	21
Suspended in his liquid orb	33
The kangaroo went on a crazy rampage	36
The ugliest animal on earth	23
Who gave the panda two black eyes	34